# HOTEL MADDEN POEMS

HOTEL MADDEN POEMS

# HOTEL
# MADDEN
# POEMS

BY PAUL PINES

CONTACT II PUBLICATIONS
New York ✦ 1991

ACKNOWLEDGMENTS: The author would like to thank *Adirondack Life*, *Contact II* and *Talisman* where some of of these poems first appeared.

*Also, George Patrick for a year in the Jacuzzi Suite;*
*Charleen Whitacre for her unflagging support;*
*Chris Shaw for his enthusiasm;*
*and Maurice Kenny for his trust.*

*Printed in the United States by Cambridge Graphic Arts, NYC,*
*on acid-free recycled paper.*



**Cover art "Main Street City Village," by Robert McGill,**
**acrylic on canvas, 1987.**

**Library of Congress Cataloging-in-Publication Data**
Pines, Paul.
   Hotel Madden poems  /  by Paul Pines.
     p.   cm.
   ISBN 0-936556-25-0 (alk. paper)  :  $7.00
   I.  Title
  PS3566. I522H67   1991
  811'. 54—dc20                           91-27147
                                           CIP

*Publication of this book was made possible, in part, with funds provided by the New York State Council on the Arts.*

*Contact II Publications, Box 451 Bowling Green, NYC 10004*

*To Carol
Charlotte
& Claude
this
fugue . . .*

## Rooming On Dream Street

At first glance, the Hotel Madden is an unremarkable brick rectangle at 22 South Street in Glens Falls, New York. But if you step back and look closely, you'll see a bowed window, a jewel in the crown of the third floor, surmounted by an odd Dutch roof. The building sits at the foot of a commercial strip composed of a lingerie shop on the line of Frederick's of Hollywood, a dog groomer, a store that traffics in Heavy Metal, the Greyhound depot at the All Points Diner and an Off Track Betting parlor. Locals call it 'Dream Street.' Nobody knows how the name originated.

At the turn of the century, Dream Street's hotels and watering holes catered to the carriage trade. Teddy Roosevelt spoke, and Lily Langtree sang, at the Empire Theater across from the Madden. Then came the loggers and factory workers with crusty bills to spend on cards, craps, horses, women and bathtub booze. Legs Diamond drove up from Albany to deal poker and Canadian hooch. On Dream Street, you could rent a room for a night or a lifetime, have your pants pressed, fence hot merchandise, get a haircut and come out smelling of Bay Rum, or melt into oblivion without a ripple.

In the 60's, when urban renewal gutted downtowns and replaced them with shopping malls, Dream Streets all across the country joined America's invisible holography: of half-remembered images lodged in the woodwork and a few old heads holding down bar stools. On the second floor where I went every day to write, I realized that in every city I'd lived—Manhattan, New Orleans, Merida, Belize—I'd found myself doing the same thing, in the same room, on the same street . . .

—*Paul Pines*

*"The man, born with only one wing, in contrast with divine creatures, makes incessant efforts to fly. In doing so he breaks his arms and legs, but persists under the banner of his idea."*

**—The Diaries of Paul Klee**

^ ^ ^ ^ ^ ^ ^ ^ ^ ^ ^ ^ ^ ^ ^ ^ ^ ^ ^ ^ ^ ^

9:00 A.M. at the Madden

Sinatra floats up
from the bar
                        on stale smoke
                        and voices
repeating
                *The Daily Racing Form*
like a Jesus Prayer

Kathy
                'Queen
                of the Quinella'
pours drinks
smiling
            as Klee did
when talking about color

"It will always possess me.
 That is the meaning of this
 Happy Hour . . ."

                        and I wonder
what odds
she'd give a century
that's aged faster than
any other
                on its way
to the finish line

^ ^ ^ ^ ^ ^ ^ ^ ^ ^ ^ ^ ^ ^ ^ ^ ^ ^ ^ ^ ^ ^

On DREAM STREET
in Glens Falls
you can

buy a pornographic video
bet on OTB
eat at PETE'S DINER

or drink at the MADDEN
a hundred-year-old hotel
where I spend my days
in a room over the bar
thinking about
what Klee
called

"Art achieved
through intuition
winged by exactitude . . ."

or is it the reverse?

The first is the way Pete
toasts my English

the second, how I eat it

^ ^ ^ ^ ^ ^ ^ ^ ^ ^ ^ ^ ^ ^ ^ ^ ^ ^ ^ ^ ^ ^ ^ ^

If what Einstein says
is true

       there is a point
       at which all things

are synchronous

time
     drops away
     and frees the senses

to perceive
    space
         from all sides
as angels
do . . .

       . . . if what Pete says
is true
          'HOLY SEE'
raised by the girlfriend
of a jockey
           named Angel
and ridden
by him

      is a sure thing
      in the 5th

```
        (   \ ~   ~ /   )
        (   \ ( 0 0 )  /   )
        (   \   ^    /   )
              =~=
```

```
^ ^ ^ ^ ^ ^ ^ ^ ^ ^ ^ ^ ^ ^ ^ ^ ^ ^
                                          ^
                                        ^~^
                                        ^~^
                                        ^~^
                                        ^~^
                                          *
                                        ===
                                        vvv
```

Mingus
  at the Five Spot
playing for all
  he can eat
Blackburn
  by the coalstove
  in McSorley's
scoring pages with
  his nerves . . .

there was
a time when poets
  and jazzmen
  built lines
like cities to live in

I grieve for it
  now in '89
my head
  a graveyard
of forgotten names
  where
      DREAM STREET
        ends
        !
    at MONUMENT SQUARE
      [!]

^ ^ ^ ^ ^ ^ ^ ^ ^ ^ ^ ^ ^ ^ ^ ^ ^ ^ ^ ^ ^

Look Ma no hands
I ever imagined

not the ones I thought
would hold me

when my own froze
in a fist or folded

like bad cards
that never pay off

but my daughter's
in the tub

conducting her first
nine months

as if her life were
a symphony
\\\\/

— — —

^ ^ ^ ^ ^ ^ ^ ^ ^ ^ ^ ^ ^ ^ ^ ^ ^ ^ ^ ^ ^ ^

My brother
convinced he is the Manhattan Creeper
responsible for abusing
old ladies on the subway

                  stares at me

in the hospital
through his medicated daze
and says

        "Whoever thought
          it would come to this?"

then lays
his head on my chest
like my daughter
or my wife

         I hold it

           Rosetta
of a hidden language

    ` `

   ` ` ` ` ] ] ] [ [ ´ ´ ´ ´
   \ \ \ \ \ \

         –  – ´ ´
       ,

       –

Job longed for
the grave

would've
preferred it

to the lesson
David

learned
throughout

his life as
King

among
The Chosen . . .

that the Lord
whose

unmediated
suffering

flows through
Creation

requires
us

blossoms of
his sorrow

to
open in praise

^ ^ ^ ^ ^ ^ ^ ^ ^ ^ ^ ^ ^ ^ ^ ^ ^ ^ ^ ^ ^ ^

Driving into Glens Falls
hometown U.S.A.

(last known whereabouts
of Gatsby—birthplace

of Bob & Ray's
Slow Talkers of America)

a guard stops traffic
to let school kids cross

the Indian Summer sun
through brittle leaves

glows on skin and hair
and I recall the way

its light looked to me
at their age against

brick apartments
in Brooklyn . . . igniting

the moment with
pure benevolent space

^ ^ ^ ^ ^ ^ ^ ^ ^ ^ ^ ^ ^ ^ ^ ^ ^ ^ ^

Einstein
   talked about
a unifying idea in nature
   the way Aquinas did
an uncreated Creator

about space
   generating itself
   out of itself
the way Nicholas of Cusa
   did a circle
        whose center
        is everywhere . . .

and now we know
   what they meant
may still be detectable
   at the moment
         of creation

as a broken symmetry
that eventually comes to rest
in a symmetry
so  sublime
   it contains
   the death
       of every atom
       and every star

and unites us
even as we speak
      *
    <*  ^  *>
     0 , 0
      *

-

-

o

Art is emotion

buried

                        in materials

as events

are in the mind

      o

      Take this ancient

      Chinese disc

      o

to hold it is

to feel a reverence

                                 embedded

                                 in the jade

continue to

exist—

     o

        that certain objects

        have been shaped

        colored

        sized and sequenced

     o

     for a blind trust

     by the senses

which have no memory

apart from

        emotion

routed

through time

     o

in patterns

that re-create themselves

in us . .


o

—

—

```
                        `
            ` ` ` ` ` ` `
              ` ` ` `
               ` ` `
                 `
\ \ \ \ \ \ \ \ \ \ \?/ / /_/ / / / / /
```

What can we say about Krishnamurti

who abandoned his destiny
as a Lama
                        to live out
                    his mortality in Ojai

or Crowley
and Gurdjieff
                    who mesmerized
their time
from cafes on St. Germaine . . .

were they merely
                        shapes
in the landscape of a century
in which so many
sensed imminent catastrophe

                                and wanted
                                to get away?

"Color possesses me,"
                        said Klee
incising his work with an ur-tongue
            of circles
            triangles & squares

```
        ^o^o^o^o^o^
          {}    {}   {}
```

PKPKPKPKPKPKPKPKPKPKPKPKPKPKPKPK

Nietzsche
              gave up
his ghost to syphilis
and brain decay
in a Jenna madhouse
dreaming
              of Salome

but left
footprints
on the turn of this century . . .


as a student in Munich
Klee
inhaled air filled
with
              self-glorification
              boundless sexuality
              and Nietzsche

but refused
ever to enter a brothel—

he died
      of scleroderma at 60
encrypting the last paintings
      with P's and K's
while stating in his epitaph:

      I CANNOT BE GRASPED
      IN THE HERE AND NOW

^ ^ ^ ^ ^ ^ ^ ^ ^ ^ ^ ^ ^ ^ ^ ^ ^ ^ ^ ^ ^

A week from Thanksgiving

news of Jorge Dalto's death

has drifted up

        the Hudson

to a place

where nobody knows his name

or his music

        that gaunt Argentine

whose fingers were tributaries

of Brazil

    and Afro-Cuba

flowing from the mother-lode . . .

        Dalto who
left records
    like Heraclitus

fragments

of visions harbored in time

held for a moment

and let go

      like a rumored

El Dorado

        a golden city

        buried

        in the mind

men find

irresistible . . .

        ask Raleigh

whose head rolled because he failed

to locate it

        in the jungles of Venezuela

or Leonardo

who modeled figures in his "Last Supper"

like puffs of smoke

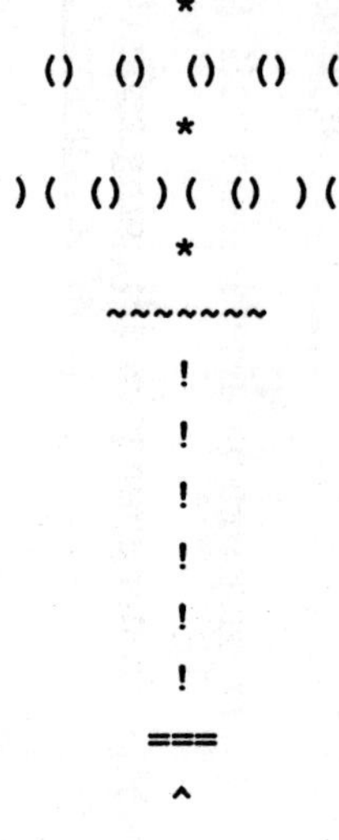

^ ^ ^ ^ ^ ^ ^ ^ ^ ^ ^ ^ ^ ^ ^ ^ ^ ^ ^ ^ ^ ^

                                        *

Tyrone Power                                    *
  a matador
by starlight
              sitting
          near a fountain                    **
          with
                  Ava Gardner                    *
                  who asks if
                  he likes music
    *
recalls
    the first bells
    he ever heard were on cows
and how
                                        *
          "I loved the song          [~~~~~~]
of the vaqueros on the ranch      { * * }
of your uncle, the Marquis"          *
                                     ***
before falling asleep                  *
    to her Spanish guitar
    weaving songs of                   *
    innocence
    & betrayal                         *

                                     \/ \/
as if they had survived
    the camera
    filmscript
    and the 50's

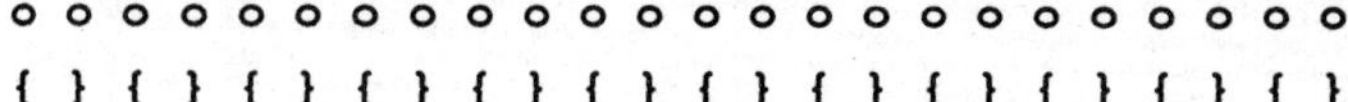

There is buried in each of us

a memory of all geometries

our glimpses of it

few and brief

are theorems

we live out in mortal detail

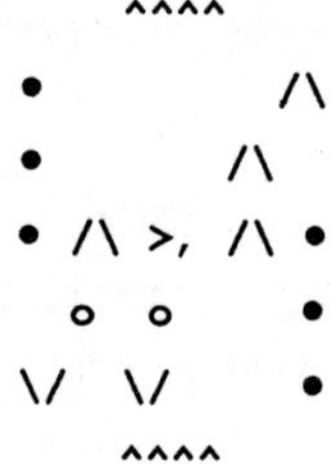

^ ^ ^ ^ ^ ^ ^ ^ ^ ^ ^ ^ ^ ^ ^ ^ ^ ^ ^ ^

A SNOWY VETERAN'S DAY

in Crandall Park
members of the
       V.F.W. Post 6199

squeeze off
a salute to fallen brethren
         lower arms
then face
the SOLDIERS MONUMENT
where the Mayor of Glens Falls
himself a veteran
gives
    his solemn word
        to raise
enough money to clean the statue
which has turned green
       and bleeds
       in the weather

streams
that run into a message carved in stone


     ooooo++++
      +++  oo
       / /
      \/ / \/

```
111111> 111111> 111111> 111111> 111111>
000000  000000  000000  000000  000000
```

Rigs downshifting
up the Northway

enter my dream
on a poem in which

I tell my brother
that I hope he won't

drive me away
or himself further

into madness . . .
that every life is

a metaphor
for suffering we

freight back
and forth like poets

trying to exit
sleep on a simile . . .

~ ~ ~ ~ ~ ~ ~ ~ ~ ~ ~ ~ ~ ~ ~ ~ ~ ~ ~ ~

My brother on a couch
in the hospital corridor

assures me he's not crazy
anymore—just pregnant

with a hidden language
that keeps him in such pain

he declines to speak
through the noun

swelling in his throat
which must be delivered

before he can repeat
the world as a verb

that moves through
every tense and person

```
        \ \ \ \ \ \ \   / / / / / / /
          ( * ) - - -   - - - ( * )
              <    } {      >
              ~  /  •  \  ~
        / / / / /  •  \ \ \ \ \ \
                •    •    •
```

^ ^ ^ ^ ^ ^ ^ ^ ^ ^ ^ ^ ^ ^ ^ ^ ^ ^ ^ ^ ^ ^

24      The Yucatec Maya drew the world
        as a lily pad

        their civilization
        built on a thin
        surface over dark aquatic life

        an image of the universe
        that also describes the mind . . .

        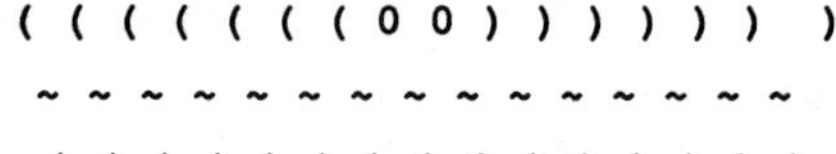

            ( ( ( ( ( ( ( 0 0 ) ) ) ) ) ) )
            ~ ~ ~ ~ ~ ~ ~ ~ ~ ~ ~ ~ ~ ~ ~
            ^ ^ ^ ^ ^ ^ ^ ^ ^ ^ ^ ^ ^ ^ ^ ^

^ ^ ^ ^ ^ ^ ^ ^ ^ ^ ^ ^ ^ ^ ^ ^ ^ ^ ^ ^ ^

I'd sooner be
            in Merida
where the bus station
smells of
            orchids
            and mangos

on a bench
full of
            Indians
            waiting for
            the millenium

than stuck
at dusk
in Newburgh
                with a ticket
                on the Short Line

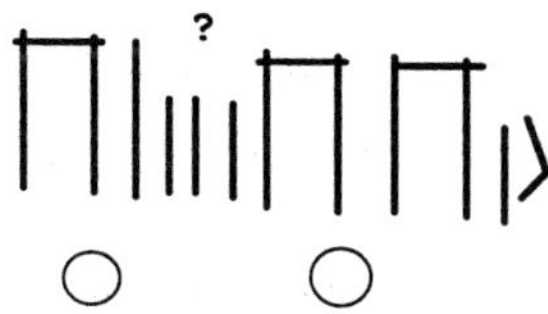

^ ^ ^ ^ ^ ^ ^ ^ ^ ^ ^ ^ ^ ^ ^

   *

There is ethyl alcohol
in interstellar space  *  the kind
you drink  *
     a whole cloud of it

*  imagine
a drunken galaxy
     *  the earth
wobbling on       *
an axis in constant motion
     *  Mars

with only
grog-blossoms to show
for aeons of belligerence
     *  Saturn
ringed by inebriate matter
hydrogen -rich
   *

     and beyond it
the farthest stars
drawn at high speeds
     by matter
we can't see
   *

     matter without light
  *

dark matter
around a milky cortex

^ ^ ^ ^ ^ ^ ^ ^ ^ ^ ^ ^ ^ ^ ^ ^

Our atoms
once composed the moment of creation

contain it still

<pre>
! ! ! ! ! ! !      ? ? ? ? ?
{  o  o  } !BANG ! {  o  o  }
    vvv                  vvv
</pre>

Ear to the wall of his equations
Einstein was deafened by the universe
solving for himself

in what
he wanted most to know . . .

DID GOD
HAVE ANY CHOICE?

) ) ) ) ) ) ) ) ) ) ) ) ) ) ) ) ) ) !

() () () () () () () () () (————) () () () () () () () ()

'meditatio dei'

Wanting
to know
who I was
I sought
myself
in you . . .

confused
I turned
to look
for you
in me

^ ^ ^ ^ ^ ^ ^ ^ ^ ^ ^ ^ ^ ^ ^ ^

Place the center anywhere
it doesn't matter

assume as the Hopi do
   it is where you are

and consider yourself
   one of the Chosen

direct the beam
   behind your eyes
   and say

               'At this point I
               interface with the universe.'

walk around it seven times
   as the people of Arabia do
   the empty casement by Abraham's temple
   believing it the center
   of creation . . .

(the Maya
   had their Kabah too)

pick a spot
   inside or outside of you

no matter

any fixed point
   will do to access
   a center

   that is everywhere

`   `   `   `   `   `   `   `   `   **[AUM]**   `   `   `   `   `   `   `   `   `   `   `

In my room breathing deeply
I feel my body stiffen and rise

through an alien will
that propels me forward

inches off the floor   A door
opens   People part   amazed

I gaze straight ahead
leaving a wake of friends

and detractors
glide down the block

still in full lotus
and into an alley

where I hope to discover
the purpose that drives

then drops me in in the snow
beside a steaming turd

~ ~ ~ ~ ~ ~ ~ ~ ~ ~ ~ ~ ~ ~ ~ ~ ~ ~ ~ ~

As Einstein sees it
we exist

        inside this universe
        like clues

        trying to piece (ourselves) together

        (into)
        a solution

        beyond the evidence
        of our senses

as I see it from
my room

           THE MOST SOUGHT
           AFTER THING
           BY OUR SPECIES
           IS DIVINE INTERVENTION . . .

                          .
                          .
                          ^
                        ^~^
                        ^~^
                        ^~^
                        ^~^
                         *
                        = = =
                       v v v

^ ^ ^ ^ ^ ^ ^ ^ ^ ^ ^ ^ ^ ^ ^

In 1905 the Hotel Madden
was fresh as a new idea
if ever men lived in ideas
or ideas were composed
of atoms or de-
composed
        the Womb of Creation
might one day be condemned
by the Fire Department
and Board of Health

Few still rent rooms
but the names of those
who've passed through
can be found in the lobby
on a plaque dedicated to

THE DREAM STREET HALL OF FAME

    Francis ''Joe'' Perscutti
    Sue ''Thumper'' Fish
    Gary ''Big G'' Estabrook
    Romeo ''Hotnuts'' Trombley
    Jim ''Jug Head'' Bond . . .

    @ @ 0 0 0 0
    ^   `   ,

    ~   0   x

^ ^ ^ ^ ^ ^ ^ ^ ^ ^ ^ ^ ^ ^ ^

What's left
of ourselves unrealized

drains back into a soup
of DNA—

our unlived lives sealed
in protein

like bottled messages
on the genetic tide


(*)

```
                    .
                    ^
                  ^ ~ ^
                  ^ ~ ^
                  ^ ~ ^
                  ^ ~ ^
                    *
                  ===
                  vvv
```

!>>>*#**#*#*#*#*#*#*#*#*#<<<

"Soon the past
will be open to my grandson"

wrote Petrarch
about books come again to light
in great libraries
of the Dark Ages . . .

                         in spite of which
Petrarch and his grandson
became the past and we are still
wise and ignorant
in the same
proportion

Ficino taught the Medici
men have two souls
                         one that ascends
another that grieves
for everything
lost . . .
            as if to illustrate
            this

poor Tasso
left the gardens of the 'Este
    to turn prematurely grey
    and die raving
    in public squares


<<<#*#*#*#*#*#*#*>>>

^ ^ ^ ^ ^ ^ ^ ^ ^ ^ ^ ^ ^ ^ ^ ^

It was 1905 in Bern
when Klee wrote in his diary

" . . . what is most intimate for me
remains most sacredly
locked up . . ."
          referring
not to love
but to

      that womb out of which
he would bear himself
             an idea
     with room enough
    for a bed and an easel

    a structure that ages
  even as it moves us
or fails to

/x/o*\
o^ o
`
~

^ ^ ^ ^ ^ ^ ^ ^ ^ ^ ^ ^ ^ ^ ^ ^

Byron
in Venice
looking out on a canal
made
      his suffering
      tributary
      to his will
with all of Europe
eavesdropping

           as it did
on Rimbaud
and Verlaine
spilling blood and semen
in a Belgian suite

but who
remembers Lafcadio
a hundred years ago
writing his way through
flops in Cincinnati
New Orleans and Martinique
as if someone cared

or me
in the tenement 60's
on Avenue B
Yuppie 80's
on DREAM STREET

these lives we inhabit
like rooms
in cheap hotels

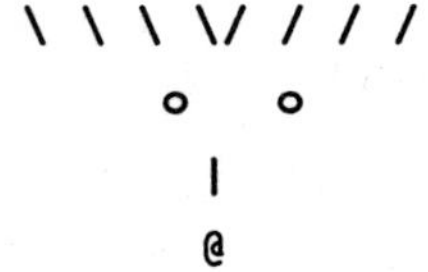

^ ^ ^ ^ ^ ^ ^ ^ ^ ^ ^ ^ ^ ^ ^ ^

In '62
Frank O'Hara said
    he hadn't yet died
    for art
but
spoke too soon . . .
       before
getting run over
by a Fire Island dune-buggy
so Alfred Leslie
could paint him
lying
      a Pietá
in the lap
     of a summer night
  *   *   his body
   /    ghostly
   ~    white
on sand
 awash with headlights

No matter what
a man does
he should
I suppose
die simply
because it's the next step
    on a journey
    he may
    or may not
    continue

like steps
outside my door
down a hall
of empty rooms
steps
I hear
have heard

behind the doors
of my life
that may be my own

< - - - - < < < < o o > > > > - - - - >
^

I am haunted also by Siquieros

the fury on the walls
of his studio
in Polanco

seas parting
for the Anti-Christ
vectors and force-fields
spinning toward Black Holes

himself
in the belly
of the Mexican night

an assassin with a paintbrush


< - - - - - < < < < o o > > > > - - - - >
v

\` \` \` \` \` \` \` \` \` \` \` \` \` \` \` \` \` \` \` \` \` \` \` \` \` \`

In 1887
when the Madden was new
Lafcadio Hearn spent
Christmas in a New Orleans
furnished room
                    reading Buddha
                    and Nerval
a poet who so wanted to make
an impression on his time
he hung himself
from a street lamp

Wanting to make an impression
also
          Lafcadio moved
to Japan and wrote
luminously
            before fading
into his century
loving Buddha
and Nerval

I shall fade from mine
at the Madden
loving Lafcadio

```
( \        / )
( \  |  / )
( 0  |  0 )
( /  |  \ )
( /        \ )
```

~ ~ ~ ~ ~ ~ ~ ~ ~ ~ ~ ~ ~ ~ ~ ~ ~ ~ ~ ~

It's that season again
Christmas bulbs lining

every house and tree
from here to Aviation Mall

Paul told the Gentiles
they saw darkly

through their bodies
though a spirit buried

in them could unbend light
make of each a beam

so radiant it might absorb
all darkness and remain

undimmed . . . Einstein
saw light mathematically

as a speed at which time
dissolved in space

but did not explain how
it moved through us or

at what rate it forged
a single prescient lens

from senses buried in
lives so clearly prismed

^ ^ ^ ^ ^ ^ ^ ^ ^ ^ ^ ^ ^ ^ ^ ^

Focusing
mind and heart

With the inner eye
and ear

to examine the moment as if            ( ( ( ) ) )
it were a map                           ( ( (^.^) ) )

this can be done anytime                ( ( ( . ) ) )
anywhere . . .                            ( ( . ) ) )
                                          ( ( . ) )
the treasure remains                        .
buried                                      .
                                            .
                                            .
                                            .
                                            .
                                            .
                                            .
                                           (X)
                                            .
                                            .
                                            .
                                            .
                                            .
                                            v
                                            .
                                            .
                                            .
                                           ( )

IMPROVISATION

^ ^ ^ ^ ^ ^ ^ ^ ^ ^ ^ ^ ^ ^ ^ ^ ^ ^ ^ ^ ^
             ^
             ^
             ^

Grasp this . . .

the soul is air
without
contour or handles
a volumeless mass
out of which
absolute knowledge opens
and closes
                  ^
What did Ives
hear in Kandinsky
or Pollock in Charlie
Parker to move
their hot lines
like Mephistopheles
faster than thought
               ^
into the fruitful decades
of this century? What
they grasped
was the way
          intelligence
shapes and unshapes
itself
            ^
An idea
almost too much
to bear

              it
was in the air
simply
              and fell
through our time
like a leaf
                    ^

                    ^

^   ^   ^   ^   ^   ^   ^   ^   ^   ^   ^   ^   ^   ^   ^   ^

If these pieces seem soft or arcane

too transparent for reflected light

to fly in the face

of Spicer's dream of a real moon

in place of the word

for moon

       or their meanings

        fade

like silent fingers

of moonlight

           let every image

           allusion

           and metaphor

I've made

be seen as originating

from a source

           that is short

almost fifty

with thinning hair

brown eyes

a vein in the forehead that throbs

under stress

an asthmatic's barrel chest

a Sephardic nose

a wife

a child

a hotel room

with a window facing north

a brother in the madhouse

a heart in the tropics

and no visible means of support

xoxoxoxoxoxoxoxoxoxoxoxoxoxoxoxoxoxoxoxoxoxoxoxoxoxoxo

*—for Charlotte
on her first birthday*

Everything my baby
sees is new

even her daddy
swollen

with the images
and attitudes

of his time
wrapped

in his
love for her . . .

a piñata
she'll open

for the rest
of her life

^^^^^^\   /^^^^^^
           `

           `

           `

^ ^ ^ ^ ^ ^ ^ ^ ^ ^ ^ ^ ^ ^ ^

More than this is given to no man

   any time

   any place

not to Buddha or Lafcadio

   Klee or Einstein

   you or me

      to feel our way through time

     alone and in the dark

not for the relief you hold up

and say

       LOOK AT ME!

     but the only kind that matters

     the kind you ride out on

       ` ` ` ` `
       { o o `
         `
        0

```
            .
         ( . )
        (   ^   )
      ( < ^ > )
     (  vvvvv  )
    (  { o o }  )
    (    \    )
     ( ( 0 ) )
  ~ ~ ~ ~ ~ ~ ~ ~ ~ ~  ~ ~ ~ ~ ~ ~ ~ ~ ~
```

Again the New Year
faces me

another hungry mouth
in the nest of this century

screaming for a piece
of my dying life

what shall I do . . .?
string hammocks on a beach

pitch my tent by the rim
of a volcano?

remain at the Madden
contained but uncompromised?

or work my way through
every bar on Dream Street

shouting like Odysseus
"Oh, God, make me a God!"

```
            '
         (  '  )
          ( ' )
          ( ' )
            '
            '
```

# *Footsteps In the Hall*

*Names in this meditation stand as metaphors shaped by ideas and feelings in the biographical context of these individual lives as I have heard them from my room.*

* * * * * * * * * * * * * * * * * * * * * *

*PAUL BLACKBURN: Troubador of East 7th for whom the sights and sounds of city and campo composed the body of the Beloved. He sang his devotions from McSorely's to Toulouse and spent his last days in the hospital listening to a recording of a mocking bird in a tree.*

*CROWLEY, a.k.a. 'The Great Beast', object of Victorian fear and ridicule, haunted the cafes of bohemian Paris and London. A rock climber who practiced the black arts and argued with Yeats over who was the better poet, he was portrayed by Maugham in "Cakes and Ale."*

*NICOLAS CUSANUS, a 15th century schoolman and early quantum thinker. Like Einstein after a unifying principle, he postulated theories (like "Deum circulum, cujus centrum est ubique," and another reconciling opposites in infinity) beyond the scope of his contemporaries.*

*EINSTEIN: a 20th Century Heraclitus.*

*FICINO, cincocento philosopher to the Medici, translated the hermetic writings into Latin and adapted late Roman philosophy, particularly that of Plotinus, to his age and profit.*

*GURDJIEFF, Beelzebub or Djinn, attracted the dying Katherine Masefield, among other pilgrim souls, to Fontainebleau, an estate outside of Paris. His esoteric 'system', designed to liberate, seems, as often, to have enslaved avatars.*

*LAFCADIO HEARN: early cultural journalist and proto-Beat whose ability to render nuance transcended muck-raking. He ended his days as a lecturer at a Japanese university, exposing the East to the Romantic poets and the West to oriental ghost stories. Like Buddha, he left footprints everywhere.*

*HERACLITUS: an early relativist who anticipated Einstein by more than 25 centuries.*

*KLEE, the Swiss painter who is to the graphic arts what his compatriot, Jung, is to psychology. From the studio of his psyche, he was moved to engage forms rooted in the collective unconscious.*

*MINGUS: A musical muralist from Watts with affinities to Siqueros.*

*NEITZSCHE: 19th century 'vitalist' who came to philosophy wielding the hammer of psychology like Thor—divined and extended cultural archetypes, i.e., Dionysus, Zarathustra, etc., but mistook them for human potentials. Driven mad by tertiary syphilis, he died raving. His legacy was further infected by the executrix of his estate, his devoted sister, a rabid anti-Semite.*

*ODYSSEUS, not Homer's but Kazantzakis', who saw, foreshadowed in the journey of this hero, the internal evolutionary process of Jesus.*

*O'HARA, poet, critic and curator who pitched his tent at the intersection of physical and psychological time where he danced like an angel to a confection of Charlie Parker, Artie Shaw and Lester Lanin. Many talk about his talent for friendship and poets still two-step on his dance floor.*

*SIQUIEROS, Mexican muralist who bungled his attempt to kill Leon Trotsky in a Guernavaca cafe, then hid out in Union Square among the abstract expressionists.*

*TASSO, poet contemporary of Dante's, with one foot in the past and other in the future. It tore him apart.*

*A* refugee from New York City's Lower East Side, **PAUL PINES** piloted the Tin Palace, a Bowery jazz club, through the '70's. There, he worked with such jazz greats as Eddie Jefferson, Richie Cole, David Murray and Joe Lee Wilson. His critically acclaimed novel, *The Tin Angel*, published by William Morrow in 1983, is based on that experience. Before that, he was a merchant seaman, a department of welfare case worker in the Fort Green and Bedford Stuyvesant sections of Brooklyn and a publicist for United Artists. He is the recipient of a 1976 CAPS grant for poetry, fellowships at MacDowell, Ossabaw, and the Virginia Center for the Creative Arts—and an 1984 artist's fellowship from the New York State Foundation for the Arts. *Onion*, his first book of poems, was published by Mulch Press in 1971. His poems, essays and translations have appeared in *New Directions*, *Prairie Schooner*, *Pequod*, *Ironwood*, *The World*, *Contact II* magazine, *American Book Review* and other literary journals. He lives in Glens Falls, N.Y., with his wife, Carol, and daughter, Charlotte.